DSARs in Education: A Practical Guide for Schools, MATs and Colleges

A safeguarding focused practitioner guide. Supporting lawful, defensible DSAR handling in education. Practical guidance for school leaders and DPOs.

By Edith McLeod
Qualified solicitor (England & Wales)

This publication is provided for general guidance and information purposes only. It is not legal advice and must not be relied upon as such. The content is intended to support professional decision making in education settings, not to replace independent legal advice or statutory guidance.

The author writes under a pen name. They are a qualified solicitor of England and Wales, but this publication is not issued in the course of legal practice, does not constitute the provision of legal services, and does not create a solicitorclient relationship.

While every effort has been made to ensure accuracy at the time of writing, data protection and safeguarding decisions are highly factspecific and depend on the circumstances of each case. The law and regulatory guidance may change over time.

Schools, trusts, colleges and other organisations should seek independent legal advice where a Data Subject Access Request raises complex, novel or highrisk issues, including those involving safeguarding, serious harm, litigation or court proceedings.

This publication is written with reference to the law of England and Wales, including the UK General Data Protection Regulation and the Data Protection Act 2018. It is not intended to address the legal requirements of other jurisdictions.

No responsibility is accepted for any loss or damage arising from reliance on this publication without appropriate professional advice.

References to the author's professional qualification are provided for context only and do not imply that this publication is regulated by the Solicitors Regulation Authority.

First published in the United Kingdom in 2026 by The Choir Press

ISBN 978-1-78963-625-3

Printed and bound by CPI Group (UK) Ltd, Croydon, CR0 4YY

DSARs in Education: A Practical Guide for Schools, MATs and Colleges

Contents

Foreword

Schools, multiacademy trusts and colleges now operate in an environment where transparency, accountability and safeguarding intersect daily. Few areas illustrate this complexity more clearly than Data Subject Access Requests (DSARs).

In theory, the right of access under the UK GDPR is straightforward. In practice, education settings face challenges that most other sectors do not: mixed data involving children and families, safeguarding intelligence, SEND documentation, professional opinions, highconflict parental disputes, staff grievances and multiagency working. Requests often arise not in neutral circumstances but at moments of heightened emotion – complaints, exclusions, family breakdown or safeguarding intervention.

This guide is written in recognition of that reality.

It does not treat DSARs as a purely administrative or legal exercise. Instead, it acknowledges that every education DSAR is also a safeguarding decision, a riskmanagement task and a communication challenge. Decisions about disclosure can affect children's safety, staff wellbeing, family relationships and trust in the institution. Mistakes can escalate conflict or expose individuals to harm; excessive caution can undermine transparency and invite regulatory scrutiny.

The purpose of this book is therefore practical rather than theoretical. It is designed to support school leaders, data protection officers, designated safeguarding leads, SENCOs, HR teams and administrators who are responsible for handling DSARs under pressure, often with limited time and resources. It explains not only *what* the law requires but *how* to apply it confidently in real education contexts.

Throughout the chapters, emphasis is placed on:

- understanding what constitutes personal data in schools
- recognising and managing mixed data
- balancing access rights against safeguarding duties
- applying exemptions lawfully and proportionately
- documenting decisions so they are defensible if challenged
- communicating clearly and professionally, even in contentious cases.

The templates and tools included in the appendix are an integral part of that approach. They are intended to move DSAR handling away from reactive, adhoc responses and towards a consistent, auditable process that protects children, staff and institutions alike.

Ultimately, lawful DSAR handling in education is not about withholding information or defensive practice. It is about providing access responsibly, transparently and safely – with the welfare of children at the centre of every decision.

About the Author

The author writes under a pen name. They are a **qualified solicitor of England and Wales** with extensive experience advising education settings on data protection, safeguarding, SEND, complaints and regulatory risk.

They have worked closely with schools, multiacademy trusts, colleges and local authorities, supporting organisations in managing complex Data Subject Access Requests (DSARs) and navigating the intersection of transparency, safeguarding duties and risk management.

Alongside legal practice, the author has acted as a **Data Protection Officer (DPO)** for education organisations, providing practical, realworld advice on UK GDPR compliance, DSAR handling and engagement with the Information Commissioner's Office (ICO).

This book reflects that experience. It is written for practitioners working under pressure, and is intended to support lawful, confident and defensible decision making in education settings, with the **welfare of children at the centre of every decision**.

Jurisdiction

This publication is written with reference to the law of **England and Wales**, including the UK General Data Protection Regulation and the Data Protection Act 2018. It is not intended to address the legal requirements of other jurisdictions.

Use in Education Settings

This book is intended to support **professional practice** in education settings. It does not replace statutory guidance, regulatory requirements or professional judgement. Safeguarding duties and the welfare of children must always take precedence.

INTRODUCTION - DSARs in Education: A Practical Guide for Schools, MATs and Colleges

---

By Edith McLeod

Schools, multiacademy trusts (MATs) and colleges operate in one of the most complex data environments in the UK. They hold vast amounts of personal data about pupils, parents, staff, governors and external professionals. Much of this information is sensitive, emotionally charged or linked to safeguarding, special educational needs, pastoral care or disciplinary processes. Against this backdrop, Data Subject Access Requests (DSARs) present a unique challenge.

Unlike many other sectors, DSARs in education often arise during conflict: parental disputes, complaints, exclusions, SEND disagreements, grievances or safeguarding concerns.

They frequently involve multiple individuals, mixed data and competing rights. Schools must balance transparency with the need to protect children, staff and third parties – all while meeting strict statutory deadlines.

This book provides a practical, legally accurate and educationspecific guide to handling DSARs with confidence. It is designed for school leaders, DPOs, DSLs, administrators and anyone responsible for data compliance in education settings. The aim is to demystify the process, reduce risk and give you the tools to respond lawfully, proportionately and efficiently.

CHAPTER 1 – Understanding DSARs in the Education Context

DSARs give individuals the right to access their personal data. In education, this right is shaped by additional considerations: parental responsibility, safeguarding duties, the Education (Pupil Information) Regulations, and the unique nature of school records. Understanding these foundations is essential before handling any request.

What counts as personal data in schools

Personal data is any information that identifies an individual. In education, this includes:

- pupil records, behaviour logs, pastoral notes
- safeguarding files
- SEND documentation
- emails mentioning a pupil, parent or staff member
- staff HR files
- CCTV footage
- assessment data, reports and teacher comments
- multiagency meeting notes
- complaints correspondence.

Professional opinions about a pupil or staff member **are** personal data. This is often misunderstood.

Who can make a DSAR

A DSAR can be made by:

- the individual themselves (pupil, parent, staff member)
- someone acting on their behalf (with authority)
- a solicitor or advocate
- a parent requesting data about their child (subject to rules below).

Requests do **not** need to mention GDPR or use formal language. A simple 'Can I see everything you hold about me/my child?' is enough.

When parents can act on behalf of children

This is one of the most misunderstood areas.

- Parents with **parental responsibility** can request their child's personal data **only if** the child is not competent to decide for themselves.
- Competence is based on **Gillick principles** – can the child understand the nature of the request and its implications?
- Many secondaryage pupils are competent; some younger children may be too.
- If a child is competent, **their consent is required** before releasing data to a parent.

Schools must assess competence case by case.

DSARs vs Educational Record Requests

These are not the same.

- Under the Education (Pupil Information) Regulations, parents of pupils at maintained schools have a separate right to access the **educational record**.
- This is narrower than a DSAR and includes only information processed by or on behalf of the school.
- DSARs cover **all** personal data, including emails, safeguarding notes and multiagency records.

Independent schools and academies are not bound by the educational record regulations, but DSAR rights still apply.

Statutory timelines

Schools must respond **within one month** of receiving the request. This can be extended by **two further months** if the request is complex. The clock can be paused while verifying identity or clarifying scope.

Schools must document any extension and explain it to the requester.

When the clock can be paused

You can pause the deadline only for:

- identity verification
- clarification of scope (if genuinely needed).

You cannot pause the clock simply because the request is large or inconvenient.

Common triggers for DSARs in education

Understanding the context helps anticipate complexity:

- parental disputes
- complaints or grievances
- exclusions or disciplinary action
- SEND disagreements
- safeguarding concerns
- staff grievances or whistleblowing
- disputes with external agencies

These contexts often involve mixed data, sensitive information and high emotional stakes.

CHAPTER 2 – Identifying Personal Data in Education Settings

Schools, MATs and colleges hold some of the most varied and sensitive categories of personal data of any sector. Understanding what *counts* as personal data – and what does not – is essential for responding lawfully to DSARs. This chapter sets out the types of information commonly encountered in education, how to recognise mixed data, and where the boundaries lie when deciding what must be disclosed.

What personal data means in an education environment

Personal data is any information that identifies a living individual. In schools, this includes both obvious identifiers and information that becomes identifying when combined with context.

Examples include:

- names, addresses, contact details
- pupil numbers, UPNs, candidate numbers
- behaviour logs, pastoral notes, safeguarding records
- SEND documentation and EHCPrelated correspondence

- staff HR files, performance notes, investigation records
- emails mentioning or discussing an individual
- CCTV footage, access control logs, biometric data
- assessment data, reports, teacher comments
- multiagency meeting minutes and referrals.

Professional opinions about a pupil or staff member **are** personal data. This includes comments about behaviour, performance, risk or wellbeing.

Mixed data involving multiple individuals

Education records frequently contain information about more than one person. This is known as *mixed data.*

Common examples:

- emails between staff discussing a pupil and their parent
- safeguarding notes referencing siblings or other children
- behaviour incidents involving multiple pupils
- staff grievance documents naming witnesses
- pastoral notes referencing family members

Mixed data must be disclosed **if** it is the requester's personal data, but thirdparty information must be redacted unless:

- the third party consents, or
- it is reasonable to disclose without consent (rare in safeguarding or conflict situations).

Schools must balance the requester's right of access with the privacy rights of others.

Professional opinions as personal data

A frequent misconception is that opinions are exempt. They are not.

Examples of personal data in opinion form:

- 'I am concerned that X is being emotionally harmed at home.'
- 'Y's behaviour has deteriorated significantly this term.'
- 'Z is not meeting expected teaching standards.'

These are personal data because they relate to an identifiable individual and express a view about them. They must be considered for disclosure unless an exemption applies.

Safeguarding records

Safeguarding data is some of the most sensitive information a school holds. It includes:

- child protection notes
- MASH referrals
- strategy meeting minutes
- risk assessments
- information from social care, police or health professionals.

This data is still personal data and is in scope for a DSAR. However, safeguarding exemptions often apply, especially where disclosure could:

- place a child at risk
- reveal confidential sources
- prejudice an ongoing investigation
- cause serious harm to the requester or another person.

Safeguarding data requires careful linebyline review.

Behaviour logs, pastoral notes and SEN files

These records often contain:

- factual descriptions of incidents
- staff observations
- pastoral interventions
- SEN assessments and support plans
- communications with parents.

All of these are personal data. They may also contain mixed data, requiring redaction of other pupils' or family members' information.

Emails and messaging platforms

Emails are one of the most timeconsuming areas of DSAR compliance.

Personal data may appear in:

- subject lines
- message bodies
- attachments
- forwarded chains
- comments in collaborative platforms (Teams, Google Classroom, MIS messaging tools).

Even a brief mention of a pupil or staff member can be personal data. Schools must conduct reasonable searches across email systems, shared drives and cloud platforms.

CCTV, access control and biometric data

Many schools now use:

- CCTV for security and behaviour monitoring
- access control systems for staff and sixthformers
- cashless catering systems using biometrics.

These systems contain personal data and must be included in DSAR searches. CCTV requests often require:

- identifying the requester in footage
- redacting other individuals
- assessing whether disclosure is reasonable or technically feasible.

Retention periods are often short, so timing matters.

Exam scripts and teacher annotations

Under UK GDPR:

- exam scripts themselves are **exempt** from DSAR disclosure
- exam marks and examiner comments **must** be disclosed
- internal teacher annotations on scripts may fall under the exam exemption depending on context.

Schools must distinguish between:

- exam scripts (exempt)
- teacher feedback (disclosable)
- assessment data (disclosable).

Multiagency records

Schools often hold information originating from:

- social care
- police
- CAMHS
- health visitors
- youth offending teams.

This data is still personal data, but disclosure may be restricted if:

- the information was provided in confidence
- disclosure would prejudice social work purposes
- the thirdparty agency objects.

Schools should consult safeguarding partners where appropriate.

Key principles for identifying personal data

- If the information is **about** the requester, it is personal data.
- If the information **mentions** the requester, it is personal data.
- If the information **expresses an opinion** about the requester, it is personal data.
- If the information **relates to an incident involving** the requester, it is personal data.
- If the information **identifies another person**, that part may need redaction.

CHAPTER 3 – The DSAR Workflow for Schools

A clear, repeatable workflow is the single most important factor in handling DSARs confidently and lawfully in education settings. Schools, MATs and colleges face unique pressures: tight timelines, safeguarding sensitivities, mixed data and highemotion contexts. A structured process protects the school, ensures consistency and reduces the risk of unlawful disclosure.

This chapter sets out a practical stepbystep model you can adopt immediately.

1. Receipt and Logging of the Request

A DSAR can arrive through any channel: email, letter, verbal request, complaint, or even a social media message. Schools must treat *any* expression of a desire to access personal data as a DSAR.

Key actions:

- Record the date and time of receipt.
- Log the request in a DSAR register.
- Capture the requester's details and the nature of the request.

- Note any immediate safeguarding or conflict indicators.

The statutory onemonth deadline begins as soon as the request is received, unless identity verification or clarification is required.

2. Identity Verification

Schools must ensure they are releasing personal data to the correct individual.

Verification steps:

- For pupils: confirm identity through school records.
- For parents: confirm parental responsibility (birth certificate, court order or MIS record).
- For solicitors/advocates: request written authority.
- For staff: verify via HR records.

If identity is unclear, the school may pause the clock until verification is complete.

3. Clarifying the Scope

Many DSARs are broad ('I want everything you hold about me/my child'). Clarification is permitted where necessary to locate the data or reduce excessive burden.

Clarification may cover:

- date ranges
- specific incidents
- types of records (emails, safeguarding, behaviour logs)
- names of staff involved

The school must not use clarification to delay or narrow the request unfairly. If the requester refuses to clarify, the school must still conduct reasonable searches.

4. Searching Systems and Locations

Education settings hold data across multiple platforms. A thorough search is essential.

Typical search locations:

- MIS systems (SIMS, Arbor, Bromcom, etc.)
- safeguarding platforms (CPOMS, MyConcern)
- email accounts
- shared drives and cloud storage
- pastoral and SEN files
- HR systems
- CCTV and access control systems
- teacher devices (if used for school business)
- paper files (archives, class folders, safeguarding cabinets)

Search principles:

- Searches must be reasonable and proportionate.
- Staff should be given clear instructions and deadlines.
- IT support may be needed for email and system-wide searches.
- Deleted data is only in scope if still recoverable.

5. Reviewing and Redacting

This is the most timeconsuming stage. Schools must review every document line by line.

Redaction considerations:

- Remove thirdparty personal data unless disclosure is reasonable.
- Remove information that could identify other pupils.
- Remove confidential sources in safeguarding contexts.
- Remove irrelevant or excessive information.
- Maintain the meaning of the document where possible.

A redaction log should record what was removed and why.

6. Applying Exemptions

Exemptions must be applied carefully and only where justified. Common educationspecific exemptions include:

- safeguarding and child protection
- serious harm to physical or mental health
- legal professional privilege
- confidential references
- management forecasting/planning
- crime and taxation (police involvement)
- exam scripts (but not marks or feedback).

Each exemption must be documented with a clear rationale.

7. Preparing the Response Pack

The response should be clear, secure and well structured.

A typical pack includes:

- a covering letter explaining the response

- a schedule of documents disclosed
- the redacted documents
- an explanation of any withheld information and the exemptions relied upon
- information about the requester's right to complain to the ICO.

Documents should be provided in a secure format (passwordprotected PDF or secure portal).

8. Communicating the Outcome

The covering letter should:

- confirm the scope of the search
- explain any redactions or withheld information
- provide the data in an accessible format
- clarify the requester's rights if they are dissatisfied.

Tone matters. Even in contentious situations, communication should remain neutral and professional.

9. Recording Decisions and Lessons Learnt

Schools should maintain a DSAR audit trail including:

- the request
- verification steps
- search locations
- redaction decisions
- exemptions applied
- communications with the requester and
- final response date.

This record protects the school in the event of an ICO complaint and helps improve future processes.

10. Managing Complexity and Risk

Some DSARs require additional oversight:

- highconflict parental disputes
- safeguardingheavy requests
- staff grievances or whistleblowing
- requests involving large volumes of email
- requests linked to legal proceedings

In these cases, schools should involve:

- the DPO
- the DSL (for safeguarding content)
- HR (for staff requests) and
- legal advisers (where privilege or litigation risk is present).

11. Building a DSARReady Culture

Schools can reduce DSAR burden by:

- training staff to write records with disclosure in mind
- reducing unnecessary email content
- using consistent templates for pastoral and safeguarding notes
- implementing clear retention schedules
- centralising key records.

A wellorganised school is far easier to search and far less likely to disclose inappropriate information.

CHAPTER 4 - Searching for Personal Data in Education Settings

Searching for personal data is one of the most resourceintensive and risksensitive stages of a DSAR. Schools, MATs and colleges hold information across multiple systems, devices and formats, often with inconsistent recordkeeping practices. A wellstructured search process protects the school from missing data, reduces the risk of unlawful disclosure and ensures the response is defensible if challenged by the ICO.

This chapter sets out a practical educationspecific approach to conducting thorough, proportionate searches.

Where Schools Must Search

Education settings hold personal data in a wider range of locations than most organisations. A lawful DSAR response requires a search across all systems where relevant data is likely to be held.

Core systems:

- **MIS platforms** such as SIMS, Arbor, Bromcom, ScholarPack or iSAMS. These contain pupil records, attendance, behaviour logs, SEN notes and communications.
- **safeguarding systems** like CPOMS or MyConcern. These hold highly sensitive data and require careful access control during searches.
- **email systems** (Outlook, Gmail, Microsoft 365). Emails are often the largest source of disclosable data.
- **shared drives and cloud storage** (OneDrive, Google Drive, SharePoint). Staff frequently store lesson materials, pastoral notes and reports here.
- **HR systems** for staff DSARs, including personnel files, investigation notes and performance records.

Additional locations:

- teacher **devices** (laptops, tablets, school phones) where staff may store notes or correspondence
- paper **files,** including safeguarding folders, SEN files, behaviour logs and archived records
- CCTV **systems** where footage may capture the requester
- access **control systems** (fobs, swipe cards, biometric systems)
- third**party platforms** used for communication, homework, behaviour management or pastoral support

A DSAR search must be proportionate, but proportionate does not mean minimal. Schools must search all locations where relevant data is *likely* to be held.

What Counts as a Reasonable Search

A reasonable search is one that is:

- **targeted** – focused on systems and locations where relevant data is likely to exist
- **comprehensive** – covering all relevant systems, not just the MIS
- **documented** – with a clear record of what was searched, by whom and when
- **proportionate** – avoiding unnecessary trawling through irrelevant systems.

Schools are not required to:

- recreate deleted data that is no longer recoverable, search personal devices unless used for school business
- search systems where it is clear no relevant data exists.

However, if staff routinely use personal devices for schoolwork, the school may need to request searches of those devices.

How to Conduct Effective Email Searches

Email searches are often the most timeconsuming part of a DSAR. A structured approach reduces workload and risk.

Use targeted search terms

Search terms should include:

- the requester's name (including variations and misspellings)
- initials

- known aliases or nicknames
- email addresses
- key incident dates
- staff names involved in relevant events.

Search across:

- inbox
- sent items
- deleted items (if recoverable)
- archived mailboxes
- shared mailboxes
- Teams or Google Classroom messages (if used for communication).

Managing large volumes

If searches return thousands of emails:

- narrow by date range
- narrow by staff involved
- exclude irrelevant systemgenerated emails
- prioritise emails likely to contain substantive personal data.

Schools must still review all emails that contain the requester's personal data, even if the volume is large.

Searching Safeguarding Systems

Safeguarding data requires special handling.

Key principles:

- Only authorised staff (usually DSL/DDSL) should access safeguarding systems.
- Searches must be conducted in a secure environment.
- Notes must be reviewed line by line due to mixed data.
- Thirdparty information (siblings, other pupils, parents, professionals) will often require redaction.
- Confidential sources must be protected.

If safeguarding partners (e.g., social care, police) have provided information, the school may need to consult them before disclosure.

Searching SEN and Pastoral Records

SEN and pastoral files often contain:

- assessments
- support plans
- communications with parents
- multiagency notes
- teacher observations.

These records frequently include mixed data and require careful redaction. Schools should search:

- SENCO files
- pastoral team folders
- behaviour logs
- intervention records
- EHCP documentation.

Searching Paper Records

Paper files remain common in education, especially for:

- safeguarding
- SEN
- behaviour
- historical records.

Search steps:

- Identify all physical storage locations.
- Search by pupil name, year group or incident.
- Check archives and offsite storage if relevant.
- Record what was searched and what was found.

Paper records must be scanned or securely copied for disclosure.

Searching CCTV and Access Control Systems

CCTV searches require:

- identifying the requester in footage
- locating relevant time periods
- redacting other individuals (often requiring specialist software)
- assessing whether disclosure is reasonable or technically feasible.

Access control systems may show:

- entry/exit times
- movements around the site
- biometric logs.

These are personal data and must be included if relevant.

Managing Staff Involvement

Staff cooperation is essential but must be controlled.

Schools should:

- provide staff with clear instructions
- set deadlines for returning search results
- remind staff not to delete or alter records
- ensure searches are conducted securely.

Staff should not decide what is or isn't disclosable – that is the role of the DSAR lead or DPO.

Documenting the Search Process

A defensible DSAR response requires a clear audit trail.

Record:

- systems searched
- search terms used
- staff involved
- dates of searches
- any systems excluded and why
- any difficulties encountered.

This documentation protects the school if the requester complains to the ICO.

Reducing Search Burden Over Time

Schools can reduce DSAR workload by:

- training staff to avoid unnecessary personal data in emails
- using structured templates for pastoral and safeguarding notes
- centralising key records
- enforcing retention schedules
- discouraging use of personal devices for school business.

A wellorganised school is far easier to search and far less likely to miss data.

CHAPTER 5
- Redaction in Practice

Redaction is the stage where DSARs in education become genuinely complex. Schools, MATs and colleges routinely hold records that contain *multiple individuals, safeguarding intelligence, professional opinions* and *information provided in confidence.* A lawful DSAR response requires a careful linebyline review of every document to ensure that only the requester's personal data is disclosed, and that the rights and safety of others are protected.

This chapter provides a practical educationspecific guide to redaction: what to remove, what to disclose, how to justify decisions, and how to avoid the common pitfalls that lead to ICO complaints.

Understanding what must be redacted

Redaction is required when information in a document relates to someone *other than* the requester and cannot lawfully be disclosed. In education settings, this typically includes:

- **other pupils** involved in incidents, behaviour logs or safeguarding notes
- **parents, carers or family members** whose personal data appears in correspondence

- **staff members**, where the information is not the requester's personal data
- **confidential sources**, especially in safeguarding contexts
- **sensitive thirdparty information** provided by social care, police or health professionals.

The key principle is that the requester is entitled to *their* personal data, not the personal data of others.

Distinguishing between personal data and thirdparty data

A common challenge is determining whether a piece of information is:

- the requester's personal data
- thirdparty personal data, or
- mixed data (information about both).

Examples:

- 'Tom pushed Jack in the corridor.'
  - For Tom: this is personal data.
  - For Jack: this is also personal data.
  - For any other pupil mentioned: redact.

- 'I am concerned that the mother is not engaging with the school.'
  - For the mother: this is personal data.
  - For the child: this is also personal data (it relates to their welfare).
  - For other family members: redact.

Mixed data must be disclosed *if* it is the requester's personal data, but thirdparty elements must be removed unless disclosure is reasonable.

When disclosure of thirdparty data may be reasonable

The law allows disclosure of thirdparty data without consent if it is *reasonable* to do so. In education, this is rare but possible.

Factors that may make disclosure reasonable:

- The third party is a professional acting in an official capacity (e.g., a teacher's name in an email).
- The information is already known to the requester.
- The third party has been copied into the correspondence.
- The information is trivial or nonsensitive.

Factors that make disclosure *unreasonable*:

- safeguarding concerns
- information about other pupils
- information provided in confidence
- information that could cause harm or distress

Schools should document their reasoning in each case.

Redacting safeguarding information

Safeguarding records require the highest level of care. They often contain:

- information from social care, police or health professionals
- confidential referrals
- risk assessments
- multiagency meeting minutes
- sensitive family information.

Redaction must protect:

- the identity of other children
- the identity of referrers or whistleblowers
- confidential sources
- information that could increase risk.

If disclosure would cause *serious harm* to the requester or another person, the school may withhold the information entirely under the Data Protection Act 2018.

Redacting emails and correspondence

Emails are one of the most common sources of mixed data.

Redaction rules:

- Remove names and details of other pupils.
- Remove personal data of parents or carers unless they are the requester.
- Keep staff names where they acted in a professional capacity.
- Remove irrelevant content (e.g., unrelated email chains).
- Remove internal discussions that do not contain the requester's personal data.

Where an email chain contains both relevant and irrelevant content, schools may:

- extract only the relevant section, or
- redact the irrelevant parts.

Redacting behaviour logs, pastoral notes and SEN records

These records often contain:

- incident descriptions involving multiple pupils
- staff observations
- pastoral interventions
- SEN assessments
- communications with parents.

Redaction must:

- remove other pupils' names and identifying details
- remove sensitive family information about others
- preserve the meaning of the record where possible.

If redaction would render the document meaningless, the school may summarise the relevant information instead.

Redacting multiagency minutes

Minutes from meetings such as:

- TAF (Team Around the Family)
- CIN (Child in Need)
- CP (Child Protection)
- EHCP reviews
- multiagency risk meetings often contain extensive thirdparty data.

Redaction must protect:

- other children discussed

- parents or carers of other children
- professionals' personal data (unless acting in an official capacity)
- confidential sources
- sensitive intelligence from partner agencies.

In some cases, the school may need to consult the originating agency before disclosure.

How to explain redactions to the requester

A clear explanation reduces complaints and demonstrates transparency.

A typical explanation includes:

- that redactions were made to protect thirdparty personal data
- that certain information was withheld under specific exemptions
- that safeguarding information may be limited to avoid risk
- that the school has provided all personal data relating to the requester.

The explanation should be factual, neutral and nondefensive.

Maintaining a redaction audit trail

A redaction log should record:

- the document name
- the type of information removed
- the reason for removal
- the exemption relied upon (if applicable)
- any consultation with safeguarding partners.

This protects the school if the requester challenges the response.

Common redaction mistakes to avoid:

- disclosing other pupils' names or details
- disclosing sensitive family information about others
- overredacting to the point of removing the requester's own data
- failing to consult safeguarding partners
- forgetting to redact metadata or document properties
- leaving redactions reversible (e.g., using highlight instead of blackout)

Redaction must be irreversible and secure.

Practical redaction techniques:

- Use professional PDF redaction tools (Adobe Pro, Redact-It, etc.).
- Avoid manual methods like drawing boxes or using highlighters.
- Always check the final PDF to ensure redactions cannot be removed.
- For paper records, photocopy and black out, then scan the redacted version.

CHAPTER 6 - Key Exemptions for Schools

Exemptions are the legal safety valves that allow schools, MATs and colleges to withhold or limit disclosure of personal data in a DSAR when releasing it would create risk, undermine safeguarding or prejudice important processes. They must be applied carefully, proportionately and with a clear rationale. Overuse of exemptions can lead to ICO complaints; underuse can expose children, staff and families to harm.

This chapter explains the exemptions most relevant to education settings, how they work, and how to apply them confidently.

Safeguarding and Child Protection Exemption

Safeguarding is the most significant and frequently used exemption in schools. It applies where disclosure would be likely to prejudice the prevention or detection of crime, the apprehension or prosecution of offenders, or the safeguarding of children and vulnerable individuals.

It applies when:

- disclosure would increase risk to a child or adult
- information was provided in confidence by a third party (e.g., a neighbour, another parent, a pupil)
- disclosure would reveal the identity of a referrer or whistleblower
- multiagency partners (social care, police, health) have shared sensitive intelligence
- there is an ongoing investigation or assessment.

How to apply it:

- Assess risk to the child or others.
- Consult the DSL and, where appropriate, safeguarding partners.
- Redact or withhold only the necessary parts.
- Record the rationale clearly.

Serious Harm to Physical or Mental Health

Schools may withhold information if disclosure would be likely to cause serious harm to the physical or mental health of the requester or another person.

It applies when:

- the requester is in a fragile mental health state
- the information contains distressing safeguarding content
- disclosure could trigger selfharm
- there is aggression or emotional instability
- the information relates to traumatic events.

How to apply it:

- Seek input from DSL, SENCO, pastoral leads or mental health professionals.
- Consider whether partial disclosure or summarisation is safer.
- Document the harm assessment.

Third Party Personal Data

Schools must protect the rights of other individuals whose personal data appears in the records.

It applies when:

- other pupils are named or identifiable
- parents, carers or family members are referenced
- staff members are mentioned in a personal, not professional, capacity
- multiagency professionals are identified in sensitive contexts.

How to apply it

Redact thirdparty data unless:

  - consent is obtained, or
  - disclosure is reasonable (e.g., staff acting in a professional role).
- Keep the requester's own data intact wherever possible.
- Maintain a redaction log.

Legal Professional Privilege

Schools may withhold information that is subject to legal professional privilege (LPP). This protects confidential communications between the school and its legal advisers.

It applies when:

- emails or documents are created for the purpose of obtaining legal advice
- communications relate to litigation or potential litigation
- notes are prepared by lawyers or for lawyers.

How to apply it:

- Identify whether the communication was for legal advice or litigation.
- Withhold the privileged content in full.
- Explain the exemption in the response letter.

Management Forecasting and Planning

This exemption protects internal discussions that relate to future planning, where disclosure would prejudice the school's ability to manage staff or organisational changes.

It applies when:

- there are discussions about potential restructures or redundancies
- there is planning for disciplinary or capability processes
- there are internal strategy discussions about staff performance.

How to apply it:

- Withhold only the parts that would prejudice planning.
- Do not use this exemption to hide completed decisions.
- Document the reasoning.

Confidential References

Schools may refuse to disclose confidential references they have given or received for staff or pupils.

It applies when:

- references are written for job applications
- references are provided to other schools or employers
- references are received from previous schools.

How to apply it:

- Withhold the reference in full.
- Explain the exemption clearly.
- Note that factual information outside the reference may still be disclosable.

Crime and Taxation Exemption

This exemption applies where disclosure would prejudice the prevention or detection of crime or the apprehension of offenders.

It applies when:

- police are involved in an investigation
- the school holds information shared by police or youth offending teams
- disclosure could compromise an ongoing inquiry.

How to apply it:

- Consult police or relevant agencies where appropriate.
- Withhold only the sensitive elements.
- Record the consultation and decision.

Exam Scripts and Assessment Exemption

Education settings must distinguish between exam scripts and other assessment data.

What is exempt:

- exam scripts (the student's written answers)

What must be disclosed:

- exam marks
- examiner comments
- teacher feedback
- internal assessment data

How to apply it:

- Withhold scripts but provide marks and feedback.
- Explain the distinction in the response.

Information Provided in Confidence

Schools often receive information from third parties on the understanding that it will remain confidential.

It applies when:

- there is information from neighbours, other parents or pupils
- there are anonymous safeguarding referrals
- there are sensitive disclosures from professionals.

How to apply it:

- Assess whether disclosure would breach confidentiality.
- Redact or withhold the confidential elements.
- Consider whether a summary can be provided instead.

How to Document Exemption Decisions

A defensible DSAR response requires a clear audit trail.

Record:

- the exemption applied
- the reason for applying it
- any consultation with safeguarding partners or legal advisers

- the specific sections withheld
- the impact on the requester's rights.

This protects the school in the event of an ICO complaint.

Balancing Transparency and Protection

Exemptions must be applied proportionately. The goal is to disclose as much of the requester's personal data as possible while protecting others and preventing harm. Schools should avoid blanket refusals and instead take a careful linebyline approach.

CHAPTER 7 – DSARs Involving Parents, Children and Disputes

DSARs in education often become most complex when they involve parents and children. Unlike most sectors, schools must navigate parental responsibility, Gillick competence, safeguarding duties, family court restrictions and highconflict situations. This chapter explains how to handle these requests lawfully and safely, with a focus on practical decision making.

Understanding who has the right to request a child's data

A DSAR can be made by:

- the **child**, if they have capacity
- a **parent with parental responsibility**, if the child lacks capacity
- a **legal representative** acting with authority
- a **courtappointed guardian.**

The school must always identify:

- who is making the request

- whether they have parental responsibility
- whether the child is competent to decide for themselves.

What counts as parental responsibility

In England and Wales, parental responsibility typically belongs to:

- the child's mother automatically
- the father if married to the mother or named on the birth certificate (post2003)
- individuals with a court order (e.g., Child Arrangements Order, Special Guardianship Order)
- local authorities with a Care Order.

Schools should verify parental responsibility through MIS records, documentation or court orders.

Assessing Gillick competence

Gillick competence determines whether a child can make decisions about their own data.

A child is competent if they can:

- understand what a DSAR is
- understand what information may be disclosed
- appreciate the consequences of disclosure
- express a clear, informed view.

Many secondaryage pupils meet this threshold, but competence is not agebased; it is casespecific.

If the child is competent:

- The child decides whether their data is disclosed.
- Parents cannot override the child's wishes.
- The school must seek the child's views before releasing data to a parent.

If the child is not competent:

- A parent with parental responsibility may exercise the DSAR on the child's behalf.
- The school must still consider safeguarding and thirdparty rights.

Handling DSARs in highconflict parental disputes

Schools frequently receive DSARs during:

- separations
- custody disputes
- disagreements over SEND provision
- complaints or allegations
- safeguarding interventions.

These requests often contain emotional or strategic motives. Schools must remain neutral and focus solely on the child's best interests and legal obligations.

Key principles:

- Do not take sides.
- Do not disclose one parent's personal data to the other.

- Do not disclose information that could escalate conflict.
- Apply safeguarding and serious harm exemptions where needed.
- Keep communication factual and nonjudgemental.

Common pitfalls to avoid:

- assuming both parents have equal rights without checking parental responsibility
- disclosing one parent's address or contact details to the other
- sharing safeguarding notes that include allegations or confidential sources
- releasing information that could prejudice family court proceedings

DSARs during family court proceedings

Family court involvement adds additional layers of complexity.

Disclosure may be restricted when:

- a court order prohibits sharing certain information
- disclosure could prejudice ongoing proceedings
- information relates to allegations still under investigation
- social care or CAFCASS has provided confidential material.

Schools should:

- check for any court orders
- consult the DSL
- consider seeking legal advice for complex cases.

Requests linked to complaints, exclusions and SEND disputes

Parents often submit DSARs when they are unhappy with:

- disciplinary decisions
- exclusions
- SEND provision
- EHCP processes
- pastoral or safeguarding responses.

These DSARs may be broad and emotionally charged.

How to manage them:

- Clarify scope where appropriate.
- Separate DSAR handling from complaint handling.
- Avoid disclosing internal staff discussions unless they contain the requester's personal data.
- Apply thirdparty and safeguarding exemptions carefully.
- Maintain a clear audit trail.

When parents disagree about disclosure

Schools may face situations where:

- one parent requests data
- the other parent objects
- the child has not expressed a view.

Approach:

- Determine whether the child is competent.
- If competent, seek their view.
- If not competent, rely on parental responsibility.
- Do not allow parental conflict to delay the DSAR.
- Consider safeguarding risks if one parent poses a threat.

DSARs made by estranged or nonresident parents

A nonresident parent with parental responsibility has the same DSAR rights as a resident parent, unless:

- a court order restricts access
- disclosure would place the child at risk
- the child is competent and refuses disclosure.

Schools must verify:

- parental responsibility
- any safeguarding concerns
- any restrictions in place.

Protecting the child's welfare

The child's welfare is the overriding consideration in all education DSARs.

Schools should consider whether:

- disclosure could cause emotional harm

- disclosure could escalate parental conflict
- disclosure could expose the child to risk
- the child understands and consents to disclosure.

Where risk is identified, the school may:

- redact sensitive information
- summarise instead of disclosing verbatim notes
- withhold information under safeguarding or serious harm exemptions.

Communicating with parents and children

Clear communication reduces conflict and complaints.

Good practice includes:

- explaining the DSAR process
- clarifying what can and cannot be disclosed
- avoiding legal jargon
- keeping tone neutral
- explaining redactions and exemptions
- signposting the right to complain to the ICO.

Summary of key decision points

Schools must determine:

- Who is making the request?
- Do they have parental responsibility?
- Is the child Gillick competent?
- Does the request involve safeguarding?

- Are there court orders or legal restrictions?
- Does disclosure risk harm?
- What thirdparty data must be protected?

A structured approach ensures lawful, safe and defensible decisions.

CHAPTER 8 - DSARs and Safeguarding

Safeguarding sits at the heart of every education setting, and it is the area where DSARs become most sensitive, most complex and most legally risky. Schools, MATs and colleges routinely hold information that is confidential, multiagency, intelligencebased or linked to risk assessments and child protection processes. Responding to a DSAR in this context requires a careful balance between transparency and the overriding duty to protect children and vulnerable individuals.

This chapter explains how to handle safeguarding information safely, lawfully and confidently.

Safeguarding information as personal data

Safeguarding records are still **personal data** and therefore fall within the scope of a DSAR. This includes:

- child protection notes
- MASH referrals
- strategy meeting minutes
- Section 47 enquiries
- CIN and CP plans
- multiagency meeting notes

- risk assessments
- information from police, social care or health
- disclosures from pupils, parents or third parties.

Even highly sensitive information must be considered for disclosure. The question is **not** 'Is this exempt?' but 'What can safely and lawfully be disclosed?'

The safeguarding-GDPR interface

Schools must balance two legal duties:

- the duty to safeguard children under the Children Act 1989 and Keeping Children Safe in Education
- the duty to provide access to personal data under UK GDPR

Where these duties conflict, **safeguarding takes precedence**. GDPR explicitly allows restrictions where disclosure would create risk.

When safeguarding exemptions apply

Schools may withhold safeguarding information where disclosure would:

- place a child or adult at risk
- reveal the identity of a confidential source
- prejudice an ongoing investigation
- undermine multiagency child protection processes
- cause serious harm to the requester or another person
- breach confidentiality owed to another child or family.

These exemptions must be applied proportionately and documented clearly.

Handling multiagency records

Schools often hold information originating from:

- social care
- police
- CAMHS
- youth offending teams
- health professionals
- early help services.

This information is still personal data, but disclosure may be restricted.

Key principles:

- The school is the **data controller** for the copy it holds.
- The originating agency's views should be sought where disclosure may create risk.
- If the agency objects to disclosure, this should be recorded and considered.
- The school must still make its own decision, but partner input is highly persuasive.

Protecting confidential sources

Safeguarding relies on individuals being willing to share concerns. Disclosing their identity can:

- deter future reporting
- place the referrer at risk
- escalate family conflict
- undermine child protection processes.

Schools must protect:

- pupils who report concerns
- parents or neighbours who raise issues
- staff who make referrals
- anonymous sources.

Where identifying details cannot be safely redacted, the information may be withheld entirely.

Managing highrisk safeguarding DSARs

Some DSARs require heightened caution, including those involving:

- domestic abuse
- forced marriage
- honourbased violence
- sexual exploitation
- gang involvement
- radicalisation
- parental mental health or substance misuse
- children in care
- ongoing police investigations.

In these cases, disclosure must be approached with extreme care.

Recommended steps:

- Involve the DSL immediately.
- Consult safeguarding partners where appropriate.
- Consider serious harm and crime exemptions.
- Document all decisions.
- Consider providing a summary instead of verbatim notes.

Redacting safeguarding information

Redaction is essential to protect:

- other children
- siblings
- parents or carers
- professionals
- confidential sources
- sensitive intelligence.

Redaction must be:

- line by line
- irreversible
- proportionate
- clearly logged.

Where redaction would render the document meaningless, a **summary** may be more appropriate.

Summarising safeguarding information

A summary may be used where:

- the original record contains extensive thirdparty data
- disclosure would reveal confidential sources
- the information is too sensitive to release verbatim
- the requester needs clarity without compromising safety.

A summary should:

- focus on the requester's personal data
- avoid unnecessary detail

- exclude thirdparty information
- maintain safeguarding integrity.

DSARs involving allegations

Where safeguarding records contain allegations:

- unsubstantiated allegations must be handled carefully
- malicious allegations may be withheld
- information about the alleged victim must be protected
- information about the alleged perpetrator must be balanced against risk.

Schools must avoid disclosing information that could escalate conflict or place individuals at risk.

DSARs involving police or social care investigations

Disclosure may be restricted where:

- police investigations are ongoing
- social care assessments are active
- disclosure could prejudice enquiries
- multiagency partners request nondisclosure.

Schools should:

- consult the relevant agency
- record the consultation
- apply crime or safeguarding exemptions where justified.

Communicating safeguarding decisions to the requester

The response should:

- explain that safeguarding information has been considered
- confirm that some information has been withheld for safety reasons
- reference the relevant exemptions
- avoid revealing sensitive details
- maintain a neutral, factual tone.

Schools should not disclose the identity of referrers or the nature of withheld information.

Building a defensible safeguarding DSAR process

A robust process includes:

- DSL involvement in all safeguarding DSARs
- consultation with partner agencies
- clear redaction and exemption logs
- documented risk assessments
- secure handling of sensitive files
- staff training on record keeping.

This ensures decisions are lawful, safe, and defensible if challenged.

CHAPTER 9 - Staff DSARs

Staff DSARs are some of the most challenging requests a school, MAT or college will ever handle. They often arise in the context of grievances, disciplinaries, whistleblowing, performance management or workplace conflict. These requests typically involve large volumes of emails, sensitive HR records and mixed data about multiple employees. The stakes are high: mishandling a staff DSAR can escalate disputes, undermine trust or expose the school to legal risk.

This chapter provides a clear, practical framework for responding to staff DSARs safely and lawfully.

Why staff DSARs are uniquely complex

Staff DSARs differ from pupil or parent requests because they often involve:

- large volumes of email correspondence
- internal discussions about performance, conduct or investigations
- mixed data involving multiple staff members
- HR processes such as grievances, disciplinaries or capability
- legal privilege where solicitors are involved
- sensitive whistleblowing information
- ongoing disputes that heighten tension.

These factors require careful handling, robust redaction and clear documentation.

Understanding what staff are entitled to

Staff are entitled to:

- their **own personal data**, including factual information and professional opinions
- emails **about them**, even if unflattering or critical
- notes from meetings or investigations **that relate to them**
- performance records, appraisals and capability documents
- grievance or disciplinary documents **that concern them.**

They are not entitled to:

- other employees' personal data
- confidential references
- legally privileged communications
- management forecasting or planning information
- whistleblowing disclosures that identify the reporter.

The challenge is separating the staff member's personal data from the personal data of others.

Searching for staff personal data

Staff DSARs often require extensive searches across:

- email accounts (their own and others')
- shared mailboxes
- HR systems
- investigation files

- meeting notes
- safeguarding systems (if relevant)
- cloud storage and shared drives.

Email searches

Email searches must be:

- **targeted,** using names, initials and relevant keywords
- **comprehensive** across inbox, sent items, deleted items and archives
- **proportionate** but thorough.

Staff DSARs often return thousands of emails. Schools must still review each email that contains the requester's personal data.

Handling HR investigations and grievances

HR files often contain:

- witness statements
- investigation notes
- interview transcripts
- internal communications
- draft reports
- legal advice.

What can be disclosed:

- factual information about the requester
- opinions about their conduct or performance
- investigation outcomes

- notes that relate to them directly

What must be withheld or redacted:

- witness identities (unless disclosure is reasonable)
- personal data of other staff
- confidential statements
- information that could cause harm or retaliation
- legally privileged material

Witness statements are particularly sensitive. Disclosure may be restricted if it would deter staff from participating in future investigations or create risk.

Legal professional privilege in staff DSARs

Legal professional privilege (LPP) is common in staff DSARs because HR matters often involve legal advice.

LPP applies to:

- emails between the school and its solicitors
- documents created for the purpose of obtaining legal advice
- communications relating to litigation or anticipated litigation.

These documents can be withheld in full. Schools must clearly record which documents are privileged and why.

Managing mixed data in staff DSARs

Staff DSARs frequently involve mixed data, such as:

- emails between managers discussing the requester and other staff
- investigation notes referencing multiple individuals
- meeting minutes involving several employees.

Approach to mixed data:

- Disclose the requester's personal data.
- Redact other employees' personal data.
- Retain context where possible.
- Avoid overredaction that removes meaning.

If redaction would render the document meaningless, a summary may be more appropriate.

Whistleblowing and confidential reporting

Whistleblowing disclosures require special protection.

Schools must protect:

- the identity of whistleblowers
- confidential sources
- sensitive allegations
- information that could deter future reporting.

Disclosure may be restricted under:

- safeguarding exemptions
- serious harm exemptions
- thirdparty data protections
- crime and taxation exemptions.

A summary may be provided where appropriate.

Handling large volumes of emails

Staff DSARs often involve thousands of emails. To manage this:

- narrow searches by date range
- use targeted keywords
- exclude irrelevant systemgenerated emails
- prioritise emails likely to contain substantive personal data
- use structured review processes.

Schools must still disclose all personal data identified, even if the volume is large.

Staff DSARs during ongoing disputes

DSARs often arise during:

- grievances
- disciplinaries
- capability processes
- whistleblowing investigations
- employment tribunal claims.

Key principles:

- DSARs must be handled separately from HR processes.
- The school must remain neutral.
- Deadlines must still be met.
- Exemptions must be applied carefully.
- Communication must be factual and professional.

DSARs cannot be refused simply because litigation is ongoing.

Communicating the outcome to staff

The response should include:

- a clear explanation of what has been disclosed
- reasons for any redactions
- exemptions applied
- how searches were conducted
- the staff member's right to complain to the ICO.

Tone is important. Even in contentious situations, communication should remain calm, neutral and transparent.

Building a defensible staff DSAR process

A robust approach includes:

- clear search protocols
- consistent redaction practices
- documented exemption decisions
- involvement of HR and legal advisers
- secure handling of sensitive files
- training for managers on record keeping.

This ensures the school can justify its decisions if challenged.

CHAPTER 10 - Responding to the Request

Once searches, reviews, redactions and exemption decisions are complete, the final stage is preparing and delivering the response. This is where everything comes together into a clear, lawful and defensible disclosure. A wellstructured response not only fulfils the school's legal obligations but also reduces the likelihood of complaints, misunderstandings or escalation to the ICO.

This chapter sets out how to assemble the response pack, explain decisions, communicate professionally and deliver the information securely.

Structuring the response pack

A clear structure helps the requester understand what has been provided and why certain information may be missing or redacted. A typical response pack includes:

- a covering letter
- a schedule of documents
- the redacted documents themselves
- an explanation of exemptions
- information about the requester's rights.

The goal is to make the response transparent, organised and easy to navigate.

Covering letter essentials

The covering letter should:

- confirm the date the request was received
- state the legal basis for responding (UK GDPR Article 15)
- summarise the steps taken to process the request
- outline the scope of the search
- explain any redactions or withheld information
- confirm how the data is being provided
- signpost the requester to their right to complain.

Tone matters: the letter should be factual, neutral and professional, even if the request arose in a contentious context.

Explaining redactions and withheld information

Transparency is essential. The requester should understand:

- why certain information has been removed
- which exemptions were applied
- how thirdparty data was protected
- whether safeguarding concerns limited disclosure.

A simple explanation might be:

> *Some information has been redacted to protect the personal data of other individuals and to comply with safeguarding obligations.*

More detailed explanations may be needed where significant information is withheld.

Providing the data in an accessible format

Schools must provide the data in a format that is:

- **secure**
- **readable**
- **commonly used.**

Most schools use:

- passwordprotected PDFs
- secure portals
- encrypted email attachments.

Paper copies may be appropriate in limited circumstances, but digital formats are generally preferred for auditability and security.

Accessibility considerations

If the requester has a disability or requires an alternative format, the school should make reasonable adjustments.

Handling followup questions or challenges

Requesters may:

- ask for clarification
- dispute redactions

- request additional searches
- challenge the application of exemptions.

Schools should:

- respond calmly and professionally
- explain decisions clearly
- avoid becoming defensive
- consult the DPO or legal advisers for complex disputes.

If the requester remains dissatisfied, they may complain to the ICO. A welldocumented process protects the school.

When to extend the deadline

Schools may extend the onemonth deadline by up to two further months if:

- the request is complex
- the school has received multiple requests from the same individual.

The requester must be informed of the extension **before** the original deadline expires, with a clear explanation of why it is needed.

When a request can be refused

A DSAR may be refused if:

- it is **manifestly unfounded** (e.g., abusive, malicious or intended to harass)
- it is **manifestly excessive** (e.g., disproportionate to the burden on the school).

These thresholds are high and must be applied cautiously.

If refusing a request, the school must:

- explain the reasons
- inform the requester of their right to complain
- document the decision thoroughly.

Maintaining a defensible audit trail

A complete record of the DSAR process should include:

- the original request
- identity verification
- clarification correspondence
- search logs
- redaction decisions
- exemption justifications
- copies of all communications
- the final response.

This protects the school in the event of an ICO investigation or legal challenge.

Reducing risk through clear communication

The way the response is communicated can significantly influence how it is received. Good practice includes:

- using plain language
- avoiding legal jargon
- being transparent about limitations

- acknowledging the requester's concerns
- maintaining a calm, neutral tone.

Clear communication reduces misunderstandings and helps maintain trust, even in difficult situations.

Bringing the process together

Responding to a DSAR is not simply a legal exercise; it is a communication task, a safeguarding task and a riskmanagement task. A wellstructured response demonstrates professionalism, protects the school and ensures compliance with the law.

CHAPTER 11 - Preventing DSAR Problems

Schools, MATs and colleges can dramatically reduce the burden, risk and stress of DSARs by improving everyday record keeping, communication habits and data management practices. Most DSAR difficulties arise *not* from the legal framework itself but from inconsistent documentation, sprawling email trails and unclear boundaries around what staff record and where. This chapter focuses on proactive strategies that make DSARs easier, safer and faster to handle.

Creating a DSAR ready culture

A DSARready culture is one where staff understand that anything they record may one day be disclosed. This doesn't mean avoiding documentation; it means documenting **professionally, factually and proportionately.**

Key elements of a DSARready culture include:

- consistent use of approved systems
- clear expectations for staff communication
- training on what constitutes personal data

- awareness that emails and notes may be disclosed
- confidence in when and how to escalate concerns.

Schools that embed these habits experience fewer DSAR challenges and fewer safeguarding or HR disputes.

Improving recordkeeping discipline

Good record keeping is the foundation of safe DSAR responses. Poorly written or scattered records create risk, confusion and unnecessary workload.

What good record keeping looks like:

- **factual, objective notes** rather than emotional or speculative commentary
- **clear timelines** of incidents, interventions and decisions
- **consistent terminology** across staff and systems
- **avoidance of unnecessary detail**, especially about third parties
- **use of approved templates** for safeguarding, pastoral and SEN notes
- **avoiding duplication** across multiple systems

What to avoid:

- personal opinions not grounded in fact
- unnecessary commentary about parents or colleagues
- storing sensitive information in personal notebooks or emails
- mixing multiple pupils' information in the same record
- informal messaging apps for school business

These habits reduce the volume of redaction required and minimise the risk of inappropriate disclosure.

Reducing unnecessary email content

Email is the single biggest source of DSAR complexity. Staff often use email as a running commentary, a place to vent or a substitute for proper record keeping.

Strategies to reduce email risk:

- Encourage staff to move sensitive conversations to secure systems (e.g., CPOMS).
- Discourage long email chains about behaviour or pastoral issues.
- Promote the use of **professional, concise language**.
- Avoid discussing other pupils or families unless strictly necessary.
- Use subject lines that reflect content clearly for easier searching.

A simple rule: *If it's sensitive, it belongs in the safeguarding or pastoral system, not in email.*

Centralising key records

Scattered data creates DSAR risk. Centralisation improves consistency and reduces search time.

What to centralise:

- safeguarding records

- SEN documentation
- behaviour logs
- pastoral notes
- complaints and investigations
- HR files
- multiagency correspondence

Benefits:

- fewer places to search
- clearer audit trails
- reduced risk of missing data
- easier oversight by DSLs, SENCOs and DPOs

Centralisation also supports better safeguarding practice and more consistent decision making.

Using templates and structured forms

Templates reduce inconsistency and help staff record information in a DSARfriendly way.

Useful templates include:

- incident report forms
- safeguarding concern forms
- pastoral intervention logs
- SEN meeting notes
- behaviour incident templates
- email templates for sensitive communication.

Structured forms guide staff to record only what is necessary and appropriate.

Implementing retention schedules

Retention schedules reduce DSAR burden by ensuring the school does not hold unnecessary or outdated information.

Why retention matters:

- reduces the volume of data to search
- minimises risk of disclosing irrelevant or outdated information
- ensures compliance with data protection law
- supports good safeguarding and HR practice

Schools should ensure:

- retention schedules are clear and accessible
- staff understand what to delete and when
- automated deletion is used where appropriate
- archived data is reviewed regularly.

Training staff to write with disclosure in mind

Staff should understand that anything they write may one day be disclosed to a parent, pupil or colleague.

Training should cover:

- what personal data is
- how DSARs work
- how to write factual, professional notes
- how to avoid unnecessary commentary
- when to escalate concerns to DSLs or managers
- how to use approved systems correctly.

This training should be refreshed annually and included in induction for new staff.

Reducing reliance on personal devices

Personal devices create DSAR and safeguarding risks.

Schools should:

- discourage staff from using personal phones or laptops for school business
- provide secure school devices where possible
- ensure staff know not to store pupil data on personal devices
- implement clear BYOD (Bring Your Own Device) policies.

This reduces the risk of data loss, unauthorised access and complex DSAR searches.

Building a proactive DSAR strategy

A proactive strategy includes:

- a clear DSAR policy
- a DSAR workflow map
- a DSAR register
- template letters and logs
- a trained DSAR lead or team
- regular audits of recordkeeping practices.

This ensures the school is prepared for DSARs rather than reacting under pressure.

The impact of prevention

Schools that invest in prevention experience:

- fewer DSARrelated complaints
- faster and more accurate responses
- reduced safeguarding risks
- fewer disputes with parents and staff
- greater confidence among leaders and administrators.

Prevention is not just about compliance; it is about creating a safer, more transparent and more professional environment.

CHAPTER 12
- Templates and Tools

Templates and tools turn DSAR compliance from a reactive scramble into a predictable, structured process. Schools, MATs and colleges benefit enormously from having readymade documents that guide staff through each stage of a request. This chapter provides a full suite of practical templates you can include as appendices or downloadable resources. Each template is designed to be adapted to your setting and used immediately.

DSAR Intake Form (1)

A DSAR intake form ensures that every request is captured consistently and that key information is not missed at the outset.

Purpose: To record the details of the request, verify identity and establish the scope.

Key fields:

- name of requester
- relationship to data subject (if applicable)
- contact details
- date request received

- method of request (email, verbal, letter)
- identity verification completed (Y/N)
- clarification required (Y/N)
- summary of request
- notes on urgency, safeguarding or conflict indicators
- assigned DSAR lead

Identity Verification Checklist (2)

Identity verification protects against unlawful disclosure.

Checklist items:

- proof of identity received (passport, driving licence, etc.)
- proof of address received
- parental responsibility verified (if applicable)
- authority from legal representative (if applicable)
- child's competence assessed (if applicable)
- verification logged and stored securely

Scope Clarification Letter (3)

A template for requesting clarification when the DSAR is broad or unclear.

Key elements:

- Acknowledge receipt of the request.
- Explain why clarification is needed.
- Provide examples of what the requester may wish to know (date ranges, systems, incidents).
- Confirm that the statutory deadline is paused until clarification is received.
- Provide a deadline for response.

Search Log (4)

A search log provides a defensible record of where and how searches were conducted.

Fields to include:

- system or location searched
- search terms used
- staff member conducting search
- date of search
- results summary
- notes on excluded systems and reasons
- any technical issues encountered

Redaction Decision Log (5)

A structured log helps justify redactions and exemptions.

Fields:

- document name
- page/section reference
- type of information redacted
- reason for redaction (thirdparty data, safeguarding, serious harm, etc.)
- exemption applied
- notes on consultation with DSL or external agencies

Exemption Justification Form (6)

A form to document why an exemption was applied.

Sections:

- exemption relied upon
- description of information withheld
- risk assessment (harm, confidentiality, prejudice to investigation)
- consultation undertaken
- decisionmaker's name and role
- date of decision

DSAR Timeline Calculator (7)

A simple tool to calculate statutory deadlines.

Inputs:

- date request received
- date identity verified
- date clarification received
- complexity assessment (Y/N)

Outputs:

- statutory deadline
- extended deadline (if applicable)
- notes on pauses or delays

Response Letter Template (8)

A professional template for delivering the final response.

Sections:

- confirmation of receipt and legal basis
- summary of searches conducted
- explanation of redactions
- exemptions applied
- how the data is provided
- requester's rights (review, complaint to ICO)
- contact details for followup

Safeguarding Disclosure Decision Form (9)

A tool for DSLs to assess whether safeguarding information can be disclosed.

Fields:

- nature of safeguarding information
- risk assessment (child, family, staff, third parties)
- confidential sources identified
- multiagency consultation
- exemptions considered
- final decision and rationale

Email Search Protocol (10)

A protocol that guides staff through email searches.

Sections:

- approved search terms
- required mailboxes (inbox, sent, deleted, archives)
- shared mailboxes to include
- how to export results securely
- how to flag sensitive content
- deadline for returning results

DSAR Workflow Map (11)

A visual flowchart summarising the entire DSAR process.

Stages:

1. receipt and logging
2. identity verification
3. clarification
4. searches
5. review and redaction
6. exemptions
7. response preparation
8. delivery
9. audit and closure

This can be printed and displayed in admin offices or safeguarding hubs.

Staff Guidance Sheet: Writing with Disclosure in Mind (12)

A onepage guide for staff to improve record keeping.

Key messages:

- Stick to facts.
- Avoid unnecessary commentary.
- Use approved systems.
- Separate pupils' information.
- Keep emails professional.
- Assume anything written may be disclosed.

DSAR - Acknowledgement Letter (13)

- reflects **statutory timescales and lawful pauses**
- separates **acknowledgement from response**
- flags **identity, scope, safeguarding and redaction** early
- uses neutral, nondefensive language suitable for education settings
- supports **a clear ICOdefensible audit trail**

DSAR Extension Notice (14)

- records lawful reasons for complexity
- applies **Article 12 (3) UK GDPR correctly**
- avoids overjustification (a common ICO criticism)
- maintains a neutral, professional tone for highconflict cases
- complements your **Timeline Calculator, Search Log and Register**

Bringing the templates together

These templates form a complete DSAR toolkit that schools can adopt immediately. They support consistency, reduce risk, and make the DSAR process more manageable for administrators, DSLs, SENCOs, HR teams and DPOs.

They also increase confidence: staff know what to do, leaders know the process is defensible, and the school can demonstrate compliance if challenged.

APPENDIX
- Full Templates and Tools for DSAR Handling in Education

DSAR INTAKE FORM (1)

Data Subject Access Request – Intake Form

1. Requester Details

- Full name:
- Address:
- Email:
- Phone number:
- Relationship to data subject (if applicable):
- Evidence of identity received: Yes/No
- Evidence of parental responsibility (if applicable): Yes/No

2. Data Subject Details (if different)

- Full name:
- Date of birth:
- Year group/staff role:
- Competence assessment required: Yes/No
- Competence confirmed: Yes/No/Not applicable

3. Request Details

- Date request received:
- Method of request: Email/Letter/Verbal/Other
- Summary of request:
- Clarification required: Yes/No
- Safeguarding concerns identified: Yes/No
- Notes on context (complaint, dispute, investigation):

4. Administration

- DSAR reference number:
- Assigned DSAR lead:
- Deadline (one month):
- Extended deadline (if applicable):
- Notes:

IDENTITY VERIFICATION CHECKLIST (2)

- Proof of identity received (passport, driving licence): Yes/No
- Proof of address received: Yes/No
- Parental responsibility verified: Yes/No/Not applicable
- Authority from legal representative received: Yes/No/Not applicable
- Child's competence assessed: Yes/No/Not applicable
- Verification completed by:
- Date completed:

SCOPE CLARIFICATION LETTER (3)

Subject: Clarification Required – Data Subject Access Request

Dear [Name],

Thank you for your request to access personal data under Article 15 of the UK GDPR, received on [date].

To ensure we provide you with the information you are seeking, we require clarification about the scope of your request. Specifically, it would be helpful if you could confirm:

- the time period you wish us to search
- any particular incidents or concerns you are referring to
- the types of records you are interested in (e.g. emails, behaviour logs, safeguarding notes)

The statutory deadline for responding is paused until we receive this clarification.

Please provide the requested information by [date]. If we do not hear from you, we will proceed with a reasonable interpretation of your request.

Yours sincerely,

[Name]

[Role]

DSAR SEARCH LOG (4)

School/Trust/College:
DSAR Reference Number:
Data Subject:
Requester (if different):

1. Search Overview

Date DSAR received:
Statutory deadline:
Extended deadline (if applicable):

DSAR Lead:
DPO/Senior Reviewer (if applicable):

Summary of scope of request:
(Include any clarification received and relevant date ranges)

2. Search Principles Applied

- ☐ Searches were reasonable and proportionate
- ☐ Searches focused on systems where relevant data was likely to be held
- ☐ Staff were instructed not to delete or alter records
- ☐ Searches were documented contemporaneously

3. Systems and Locations Searched

System/ Location	Description (e.g. purpose of system)	Search Terms Used	Date Range Applied	Staff Member	Date Completed	Results Summary
MIS (e.g. SIMS/ Arbor/ Bromcom)	Pupil/staff core records					
Safeguarding system (e.g. CPOMS/ MyConcern)	Safeguarding concerns and referrals					
SEN/Pastoral files	SENCO and pastoral records					

4. Email Search Detail (if applicable)

Mailboxes searched:

- ☐ Requester
- ☐ Named staff
- ☐ Shared mailboxes

Search terms used:
(names, initials, email addresses, aliases, key dates)

Date range applied:

Volume returned:
(approximate – e.g. 'c. 1,200 emails')

Approach to managing volume:

- ☐ Narrowed by date
- ☐ Narrowed by staff involved
- ☐ Excluded systemgenerated emails
- ☐ Prioritised substantive content

5. Safeguarding System Search

Accessed by:

☐ DSL ☐ DDSL

Search parameters:

Thirdparty data identified: ☐ Yes ☐ No

Confidential sources identified: ☐ Yes ☐ No

Consultation required with external agencies: ☐ Yes ☐ No

Details:

6. Paper Record Searches

Locations searched:
(cabinets, archives, offsite storage)

Method:

- ☐ Manual review
- ☐ Scanned copies created

Results summary:

7. Systems Not Searched

System/Location	Reason Not Searched

(Only include where it was clear no relevant data could be held.)

8. Issues or Limitations Encountered

☐ Access restrictions
☐ Technical limitations
☐ Records no longer retained
☐ Data deleted prior to DSAR receipt

Details:

9. Confirmation

I confirm that the searches recorded above were conducted in accordance with the school's/trust's DSAR procedure and reflect reasonable and proportionate efforts to locate personal data relevant to this request.

Completed by:
Name:
Role:
Signature:
Date:

DSAR REDACTION DECISION LOG (5)

School/Trust/College:
DSAR Reference Number:
Data Subject:
Requester (if different):

1. Document Details

Document Reference	Document Title/ Description	Source System (e.g. CPOMS, email, MIS)	Date of Document

2. Redaction Decision Record

Page/ Section	Information Redacted	Category of Information	Reason for Redaction	Exemption Relied Upon	Decision-maker
		☐ Thirdparty personal data ☐ Safeguarding ☐ Confidential source ☐ Legal advice ☐ Other			

3. Nature of Redacted Information

(Complete for each redaction or group of redactions.)

- ☐ Other pupil(s') personal data
- ☐ Parent/family member personal data
- ☐ Staff personal data (nonprofessional capacity)
- ☐ Safeguarding intelligence

- ☐ Confidential referrer or whistleblower
- ☐ Information provided by external agency
- ☐ Legally privileged material
- ☐ Information irrelevant to the data subject

Additional details:

4. Reasonableness and Balancing Assessment

In deciding to redact this information, the following factors were considered:

- ☐ Whether the information constitutes thirdparty personal data
- ☐ Whether the third party has consented to disclosure
- ☐ Whether disclosure would be reasonable without consent
- ☐ Whether disclosure could cause harm or distress
- ☐ Whether disclosure would compromise safeguarding
- ☐ Whether disclosure would reveal a confidential source
- ☐ Whether redaction preserves the meaning of the document

Summary of balancing assessment:

5. Safeguarding Considerations (if applicable)

- ☐ Disclosure could place a child at risk
- ☐ Disclosure could place another individual at risk
- ☐ Disclosure could undermine safeguarding processes
- ☐ Disclosure could escalate conflict or cause serious harm

DSL consulted: ☐ Yes ☐ No
Summary of DSL input:

6. External Consultation (if applicable)

☐ Social care
☐ Police
☐ Health professionals
☐ Legal advisers
☐ Other agency (specify)

Summary of consultation and outcome:

7. Decision Outcome

☐ Information redacted and disclosed in part
☐ Information withheld in full
☐ Information summarised instead of disclosed verbatim

Where summarisation is used, confirm summary prepared separately:

☐ Yes ☐ No

8. Redaction Method

☐ Professional PDF redaction tool used
☐ Redaction checked and confirmed irreversible
☐ Metadata reviewed and cleared

9. Confirmation

I confirm that the redaction decisions recorded above were made in accordance with the school's/trust's DSAR procedure and reflect a lawful, proportionate, and defensible approach to disclosure.

Completed by:
Name:
Role:
Signature:
Date:

10. Review and SignOff

Reviewed by (DSAR Lead/DPO):
Name:
Role:
Date:

- ☐ Redaction decisions approved
- ☐ Further review required (details below)

DSAR EXEMPTION JUSTIFICATION FORM (6)

School/Trust/College:
DSAR Reference Number:

Data Subject:
Requester (if different):

Decisionmaker:
Role:
Date of decision:

1. Exemption Relied Upon

(Select all that apply.)

- ☐ Safeguarding/child protection
- ☐ Serious harm to physical or mental health
- ☐ Thirdparty personal data
- ☐ Legal professional privilege
- ☐ Confidential reference
- ☐ Crime and taxation
- ☐ Exam script exemption
- ☐ Information provided in confidence
- ☐ Management forecasting/planning

2. Description of Information Affected

(Provide a clear, specific description of the information to which the exemption is applied. Do not reproduce the content itself.)

3. Nature of Restriction Applied

- ☐ Information withheld in full
- ☐ Information redacted and disclosed in part
- ☐ Information summarised instead of disclosed verbatim

If summarisation is used, confirm summary prepared separately:

☐ Yes ☐ No

4. Risk Assessment

In applying this exemption, the following risks were identified:

- ☐ Disclosure would be likely to place a child at risk
- ☐ Disclosure would be likely to place another individual at risk
- ☐ Disclosure would reveal a confidential source
- ☐ Disclosure would prejudice an ongoing investigation
- ☐ Disclosure would undermine safeguarding or multiagency processes
- ☐ Disclosure would cause serious harm to physical or mental health
- ☐ Disclosure would breach the rights of a third party
- ☐ Disclosure would prejudice legal proceedings or legal advice

Details/explanation:

5. Proportionality and Balancing Assessment

In deciding to apply this exemption, the following factors were considered:

- ☐ The data subject's right of access under UK GDPR
- ☐ The nature and sensitivity of the information

- ☐ The impact of disclosure on the data subject
- ☐ The impact of disclosure on other individuals
- ☐ Whether partial disclosure or redaction would sufficiently mitigate risk
- ☐ Whether summarisation could provide meaningful access without creating risk

Summary of balancing assessment:

(Explain why applying the exemption is necessary and proportionate in this case.)

6. Safeguarding Considerations (if applicable)

- ☐ DSL consulted
- ☐ Deputy DSL consulted

Name and role of safeguarding lead consulted:

Summary of safeguarding advice received:

7. External Consultation (if applicable)

- ☐ Social care
- ☐ Police
- ☐ Health professionals
- ☐ Legal advisers
- ☐ Other agency (specify):

Summary of consultation and outcome:

8. Decision Outcome

- ☐ Exemption applied as justified above
- ☐ Further review required
- ☐ Escalated for legal advice

Final decision and rationale:
(Confirm why the exemption is lawful, necessary and defensible.)

9. Confirmation

I confirm that this exemption decision has been made in accordance with the school's/trust's DSAR procedure, reflects a lawful and proportionate application of the UK GDPR and Data Protection Act 2018, and has been documented to support audit and regulatory scrutiny.

Signed:
Name:
Role:
Signature:
Date:

10. Review and SignOff

Reviewed by (DSAR Lead/DPO):
Name:
Role:
Date:

- ☐ Decision approved
- ☐ Further action required (details below)

DSAR TIMELINE CALCULATOR AND RECORD (7)

School/Trust/College:
DSAR Reference Number:

Data Subject:
Requester (if different):

1. Initial Receipt of Request

Date DSAR received:
Method of request: ☐ Email ☐ Letter ☐ Verbal ☐ Other

☐ equest recognised as a DSAR on receipt

Statutory onemonth deadline (initial):
(Calculate from the date of receipt.)

2. Identity Verification

Identity verification required: ☐ Yes ☐ No

If yes:

Date verification requested:
Date verification completed:

☐ Statutory clock paused pending identity verification

Revised deadline following verification:

3. Scope Clarification

Scope clarification required: ☐ Yes ☐ No

If yes:

Date clarification requested:
Date clarification received:

- ☐ Statutory clock paused pending clarification

Revised deadline following clarification:

4. Complexity Assessment

Request assessed as complex: ☐ Yes ☐ No

(Complexity indicators may include volume of data, mixed data, safeguarding content, staff records, or multisystem searches.)

Date complexity assessment completed:
Completed by (DSAR Lead/DPO):

5. Extension of Deadline

Extension applied: ☐ Yes ☐ No

If yes:

- **Statutory basis:** Article 12(3) UK GDPR
- **Reason for extension:**
  ☐ Volume of data
  ☐ Mixed data involving multiple individuals

☐ Safeguarding or SEN records
☐ Extensive email searches
☐ Other (specify):

- **Date extension notice issued:**
- **Extended deadline (up to two further months):**

6. Final Calculated Deadline

- **Final statutory deadline for response:**

☐ Deadline communicated to requester
☐ Deadline recorded in DSAR register

7. Response Issued

Date response sent:

☐ Response issued within statutory timeframe
☐ Response issued following lawful extension

- If not within timeframe, explanation:

8. Confirmation and Audit Trail

- I confirm that the DSAR timeline above has been calculated and recorded in accordance with UK GDPR statutory requirements and the school's/trust's DSAR procedure.

- **Completed by:**
  Name:
  Role:
  Signature:
  Date:

9. Review and SignOff

Reviewed by (DSAR Lead/DPO):
Name:
Role:
Date:

- ☐ Timeline confirmed as accurate
- ☐ Further review required (details below)

DATA SUBJECT ACCESS REQUEST - RESPONSE LETTER (8)

[School/Trust/College Letterhead]

Date: [dd/mm/yyyy]
Private and Confidential

Dear [Name],

Response to Data Subject Access Request

Thank you for your Data Subject Access Request ('DSAR') received on **[date]**.

We have now completed our consideration of your request and provide this response in accordance with **Article 15 of the UK General Data Protection Regulation and the Data Protection Act 2018.**

1. Identity and Scope

Before responding to your request, we verified your identity and, where relevant, your authority to act on behalf of another individual.

Your request was understood to relate to the following scope:

- **Data subject:** [name]
- **Relevant time period:** [dates]
- **Types of records:** [e.g. emails, safeguarding records, SEN files, HR records]

Where clarification was required, this was sought and taken into account before searches were undertaken.

2. Searches Undertaken

We carried out **reasonable and proportionate searches** across systems where personal data relating to the data subject was likely to be held. These included, where applicable:

- management information systems;
- safeguarding and pastoral records;
- SEN and support files;
- email and shared storage systems;
- paper records and archives;
- CCTV or accesscontrol systems.

The scope and outcome of these searches have been documented internally in line with our DSAR procedure.

3. Personal Data Disclosed

Enclosed with this letter is a copy of the **personal data we hold relating to [you/your child]**, identified through the searches described above.

The information is provided in a secure format.

4. Redactions and Withheld Information

Some information has been **redacted or withheld** from the disclosed material.

This is because certain content:

- contains **personal data relating to other individuals;**
- relates to **safeguarding or child protection matters;**
- was provided in confidence or would reveal confidential sources;
- is subject to **legal professional privilege**; or
- falls within another lawful exemption under the Data Protection Act 2018.

Redactions have been applied **line by line** and only where necessary. Where appropriate, information has been summarised rather than disclosed verbatim.

5. Safeguarding Considerations

Where safeguarding information is involved, disclosure decisions have been made with the **welfare of children as the overriding consideration**.

In some cases, information has been limited or withheld where disclosure would be likely to:

- place a child or another individual at risk;
- undermine safeguarding or multiagency processes; or
- cause serious harm.

These decisions have been made in consultation with the Designated Safeguarding Lead, and where appropriate, with external safeguarding partners.

6. Exemptions Applied

Where information has been withheld, this has been done in reliance on one or more of the following lawful exemptions:

- safeguarding and child protection;
- serious harm to physical or mental health;
- thirdparty personal data;
- legal professional privilege;
- confidential references;
- crime and taxation;
- exam script exemption.

Each exemption has been applied **proportionately** and documented to ensure the decisionmaking process is lawful and defensible.

7. Your Rights

If you are dissatisfied with this response, you have the right to:

- request a review of our handling of your DSAR; and/or
- complain to the **Information Commissioner's Office (ICO).**

Further information about your rights is available at **www.ico.org.uk**.

If you have any questions about this response, please contact **[DSAR Lead/DPO contact details]**, quoting the reference number above.

Yours sincerely,

[Name]
[Role]
[School/Trust/College]
[Contact details]

SAFEGUARDING DISCLOSURE DECISION FORM (9)

(For Use in DSAR Handling)

School/Trust/College:
DSAR Reference Number:

Data Subject:
Requester (if different):

DSL/Decisionmaker:

Role:
Date of decision:

1. Nature of Safeguarding Information

Type of safeguarding information involved:

- ☐ Child protection records
- ☐ Safeguarding concern notes
- ☐ Referrals to social care/MASH
- ☐ Strategy meeting minutes
- ☐ Risk assessments
- ☐ Multiagency correspondence
- ☐ Other (specify):

Source of information:

- ☐ School staff
- ☐ Pupil
- ☐ Parent/carer
- ☐ Social care
- ☐ Police
- ☐ Health professional
- ☐ Other (specify):

2. Data Subject Relationship

The safeguarding information relates to:

- ☐ The data subject directly
- ☐ The data subject and other children (mixed data)
- ☐ The data subject and other family members
- ☐ Thirdparty individuals only (contextual relevance)

3. Risk Assessment if Disclosed

Disclosure of this information would be likely to:

- ☐ Place a child at risk
- ☐ Place another individual at risk
- ☐ Escalate family or parental conflict
- ☐ Undermine safeguarding or child protection processes
- ☐ Reveal the identity of a confidential source
- ☐ Prejudice an ongoing investigation or assessment
- ☐ Cause serious harm to physical or mental health

Details of identified risks:
(Include who may be harmed and how.)

4. Confidential Sources

- ☐ Information was provided in confidence
- ☐ Identity of referrer/whistleblower identified
- ☐ Anonymous source involved

If yes, details (do not name source):

5. MultiAgency Considerations

- ☐ Information originated from another agency
- ☐ Consultation required prior to disclosure

Agencies consulted (if applicable):

- ☐ Social care
- ☐ Police
- ☐ Health professionals
- ☐ Other (specify):

Summary of consultation and views expressed:

6. Disclosure Options Considered

The following options were considered:

- ☐ Full disclosure
- ☐ Partial disclosure with redactions
- ☐ Provision of a summary instead of original records
- ☐ Withholding information under safeguarding/serious harm exemption

Reason full disclosure is not appropriate (if applicable):

7. Decision Outcome

- ☐ Information disclosed in full
- ☐ Information disclosed with redactions
- ☐ Summary provided instead of verbatim records
- ☐ Information withheld in full

Legal basis/exemption relied upon:

- ☐ Safeguarding/child protection
- ☐ Serious harm to physical or mental health
- ☐ Thirdparty personal data
- ☐ Information provided in confidence

8. Rationale for Decision

(Explain clearly why this decision is necessary, proportionate, and in the best interests of safeguarding, while balancing the data subject's right of access.)

9. Recording and Communication

- ☐ Decision recorded in DSAR file
- ☐ Linked redaction/exemption logs completed
- ☐ Decision reflected accurately in DSAR response letter

10. Confirmation

I confirm that this safeguarding disclosure decision has been made with the **welfare of children as the overriding consideration**, in accordance with the school's/trust's safeguarding duties and data protection obligations.

Signed (DSL/Decisionmaker):
Name:
Role:
Signature:
Date:

11. Review and SignOff (if applicable)

Reviewed by (DPO/Senior Leader):
Name:
Role:
Date:

- ☐ Decision approved
- ☐ Further action required (details below)

EMAIL SEARCH PROTOCOL FOR DSARS (10)

School/Trust/College:
DSAR Reference Number:

Data Subject:
Relevant date range

Issued by (DSAR Lead/DPO):
Date issued:

1. Purpose of This Protocol

This protocol sets out how email searches must be conducted in response to a **Data Subject Access Request (DSAR).**

Its purpose is to ensure that:

- searches are **reasonable and proportionate;**
- all relevant personal data is identified;
- records are preserved and not altered; and
- the organisation can demonstrate **a clear audit trail** if challenged.

Staff are responsible for **identifying and returning potentially relevant material**, not for deciding what is disclosable.

2. Scope of Email Searches

Email searches must be conducted across all email systems **where relevant data is likely to be held**, which may include:

- ☐ Individual staff inboxes
- ☐ Sent items
- ☐ Deleted items (where still recoverable)
- ☐ Archived mailboxes
- ☐ Shared mailboxes
- ☐ Group or functional mailboxes
- ☐ Messaging platforms used for school business (e.g. Teams messages, where applicable)

Personal devices or accounts must **only** be searched where they are routinely used for school business.

3. Search Terms to Be Used

Staff must use the following search terms as a minimum:

- the data subject's full name;
- known name variations or misspellings;
- initials;
- email addresses;
- pupil ID numbers (where applicable);
- key incident dates;
- names of staff directly involved in relevant events

Additional terms may be specified by the DSAR Lead where appropriate.

4. Date Range

Searches must be limited to the following date range unless otherwise instructed:

From:
To:

Staff must not narrow the date range without authorisation from the DSAR Lead.

5. Managing Large Volumes of Emails

Where searches return a high volume of results:

- ☐ Apply the agreed date range
- ☐ Prioritise emails likely to contain substantive personal data
- ☐ Exclude routine systemgenerated messages where clearly irrelevant
- ☐ Do not exclude emails solely because they are informal or internal

All emails containing personal data relating to the data subject **must be returned**, regardless of tone or content.

6. Preservation of Records

Staff must:

- **not delete, edit, forward, or amend** any emails once a DSAR is known;
- ensure that potentially relevant emails are preserved;
- report immediately if records may have been deleted prior to the DSAR being received.

Any known limitations must be documented.

7. Safeguarding and Sensitive Content

Emails may contain:

- safeguarding information;
- sensitive family or thirdparty data;
- confidential sources;
- professional opinions.

Staff must **not withhold** emails on this basis. All potentially relevant emails must be returned securely to the DSAR Lead, who will manage safeguarding, redaction, and exemption decisions.

8. Returning Search Results

Emails must be returned to the DSAR Lead by **[date]** using the approved secure method.

☐ Exported securely
☐ Clearly labelled
☐ Not edited or annotated

Staff must confirm:

- which folders were searched;
- which search terms were used;
- the approximate volume of emails returned.

9. Declaration by Staff Member

I confirm that I have conducted email searches in accordance with this protocol and have returned all potentially relevant material identified.

- **Name:**
  Role:
  Email account(s) searched:

Date search completed:
Signature:

10. DSAR Lead Review

- **Reviewed by (DSAR Lead/DPO):**
  Date:
- ☐ Searches adequate
  ☐ Further searches required (details below)

DSAR WORKFLOW MAP (EDUCATION SETTINGS) (11)

Stage 1 – Receipt and Recognition of Request

Trigger:
Any written or verbal request that expresses a wish to access personal data.

Key actions:

- Recognise the request as a DSAR (no formal wording required).
- Record date and method of receipt.
- Log request in DSAR register.
- Allocate DSAR reference number.
- Identify any immediate safeguarding, conflict, or legal risk indicators.

Outcome:
Statutory onemonth deadline starts (subject to lawful pauses).

Stage 2 – Identity and Authority Verification

Decision point:
Is the identity and authority of the requester clear?

Key actions:

- Verify identity of the requester.
- Verify parental responsibility or authority to act (if applicable).
- Assess child competence (Gillick) where a parent is requesting a child's data.
- Pause the statutory clock if verification is required.

Outcome:
Proceed once identity and authority are confirmed.

Stage 3 – Scope Clarification (If Required)

Decision point:
Is the request clear and reasonably scoped?

Key actions:

- Assess whether clarification is genuinely required to locate data.
- Request clarification (dates, systems, incidents) if necessary.
- Pause the statutory clock pending clarification.
- Record clarification received.

Outcome:
Define final scope and date range for searches.

Stage 4 – Complexity Assessment

Decision point:
Is the request complex?

Complexity indicators include:

- Large volumes of data
- Mixed data involving multiple individuals
- Safeguarding or SEN records
- Extensive email searches
- Staff DSARs or legal proceedings

Key actions:

- Assess complexity.
- Decide whether a lawful extension is required.
- Issue extension notice if applicable.

Outcome:
Confirmed statutory deadline (original or extended).

Stage 5 – Searches for Personal Data

Key actions:

- Identify all systems where relevant data is likely to be held.
- Issue search instructions to staff (including email search protocol).
- Conduct proportionate searches across:
- MIS systems
- Safeguarding platforms
- SEN and pastoral files
- Email systems and shared drives
- HR systems (if staff DSAR)
- Paper records
- CCTV or accesscontrol systems
- Document searches in DSAR Search Log.

Outcome:
All potentially relevant personal data gathered for review.

Stage 6 – Review and Redaction

Key actions:

- Review documents line by line.

- Identify the data subject's personal data.
- Identify thirdparty personal data.
- Redact thirdparty information unless disclosure is reasonable.
- Preserve the meaning of documents where possible.
- Record decisions in Redaction Decision Log.

Outcome:
Redacted disclosure set prepared.

Stage 7 – Safeguarding Assessment (If Applicable)

Decision point:
Does the data include safeguarding information?

Key actions:

- Refer safeguarding material to the DSL.
- Assess risk of harm if disclosed.
- Identify confidential sources or multiagency intelligence.
- Consult external agencies where appropriate.
- Decide whether to:
- disclose,
- redact,
- summarise, or
- withhold safeguarding information.
- Record decisions in Safeguarding Disclosure Decision Form.

Outcome:
Safeguardingsafe disclosure approach confirmed.

Stage 8 – Exemptions Assessment

Key actions:

- Identify applicable exemptions (e.g. safeguarding, serious harm, thirdparty data, legal privilege).
- Apply exemptions narrowly and proportionately.
- Consider partial disclosure or summarisation first.
- Complete Exemption Justification Form.

Outcome:
Lawful basis for any withheld information documented.

Stage 9 – Response Preparation

Key actions:

- Compile response pack:
- Covering letter
- Schedule of documents (if used)
- Redacted documents and/or summaries
- Ensure secure format (passwordprotected PDF or secure portal).
- Final quality check for completeness and accuracy.

Outcome:
Final DSAR response ready for issue.

Stage 10 – Issue Response

Key actions:

- Issue response within statutory deadline.
- Provide information securely.

- Include explanation of redactions and exemptions.
- Signpost right to complain to the ICO.

Outcome:
DSAR formally completed.

STAFF GUIDANCE: WRITING AND WORKING WITH RECORDS IN DSARREADY EDUCATION SETTINGS (12)

Why This Matters

Schools and colleges are required by law to respond to **Data Subject Access Requests (DSARs).** This means that **records you create may be disclosed** to pupils, parents, or staff members.

Good recordkeeping protects:

- children and families,
- staff professionalism and wellbeing, and
- the school or trust as an organisation.

Key Principles for Staff

1. Stick to Facts

- Record what happened, **when, where, and who was involved.**
- Avoid speculation, assumptions, or emotive language.
- Distinguish clearly between **fact and professional opinion.**

✓ 'Pupil left the classroom without permission at 10:15am.'
× 'Pupil was being deliberately disruptive.'

2. Be Professional at All Times

Write every record as if it **may be read by the individual concerned.**

Avoid sarcasm, frustration, or informal commentary.

Do not use email or messages to 'vent'.

3. Record Only What Is Necessary

- Avoid unnecessary detail, particularly about:
- parents or family members;
- other pupils;
- staff opinions unrelated to safeguarding or education.
- Do not duplicate the same information across multiple systems.

4. Keep Pupils' Information Separate

- Do not record information about **multiple pupils in the same note** unless unavoidable.
- Where incidents involve more than one pupil, ensure records are **clearly separated.**

This reduces redaction and protects thirdparty privacy.

5. Use Approved Systems

Record safeguarding, pastoral, and SEN information **only in approved systems** (e.g. safeguarding platforms, MIS).

Avoid storing personal data:

- in personal notebooks;
- on personal devices;
- in informal messaging apps.

6. Be Careful with Email

Email is one of the **largest sources of DSAR disclosures.**

Good practice:

- Keep emails factual and concise.
- Avoid long email chains discussing behaviour or concerns.
- Move sensitive matters to secure systems as soon as possible.

A simple rule:
If it's sensitive, it probably doesn't belong in email.

7. Safeguarding Information Requires Extra Care

- Safeguarding records are still personal data and may be requested.
- Never promise confidentiality to a pupil or parent.
- Do not identify referrers or confidential sources in general correspondence.

Safeguarding decisions about disclosure are made by the **Designated Safeguarding Lead (DSL)**, not individual staff.

8. Do Not Delete or Alter Records

Once you are aware of a DSAR:

- Do not **delete, edit, or amend records**.
- Preserve all relevant information.
- Follow any search instructions issued by the DSAR Lead.

If You Are Asked to Help with a DSAR

You may be asked to:

- search your email or files;
- return potentially relevant material.

You must:

- follow the search instructions provided;
- return **all potentially relevant information**, even if sensitive or unflattering;
- **not decide** what should or should not be disclosed.

Disclosure decisions are made centrally by the DSAR Lead, DSL, or DPO.

Key Reminder

Anything you write may one day be disclosed.

Professional, factual recordkeeping is not about withholding information – it is about protecting children, staff, and the school by ensuring records are accurate, proportionate, and defensible.

DATA SUBJECT ACCESS REQUEST - ACKNOWLEDGEMENT LETTER (13)

[School/Trust/College Letterhead]

Date: [dd/mm/yyyy]
Private and Confidential

Dear [Name],

Acknowledgement of Data Subject Access Request

We acknowledge receipt of your **Data Subject Access Request ('DSAR')** received on **[date]**.

This request is being processed in accordance with **Article 15 of the UK General Data Protection Regulation** and **the Data Protection Act 2018.**

1. Statutory Timescale

We will respond to your request **within one month** of the date of receipt. Based on the date above, the current statutory deadline for response is **[date]**, unless one of the following applies:

- we require further information to verify identity or authority;
- clarification of the scope of your request is necessary; or
- the request is assessed as complex and a lawful extension is applied.

Where the statutory deadline is paused or extended, we will notify you in writing.

2. Identity and Authority Verification

Before releasing any personal data, we are required to verify the identity of the requester and, where relevant, their authority to act on behalf of another individual.

If additional verification is required, we will contact you separately. The statutory deadline will be paused until verification is completed.

3. Scope of the Request

If your request is broad or unclear, we may ask you to clarify the scope (for example, by confirming relevant time periods, systems, or specific incidents). This helps ensure that searches are reasonable, proportionate, and accurate.

If clarification is required, we will write to you separately. Until clarification is received, the statutory deadline may be paused.

4. Searches and Review Process

Once identity and scope are confirmed, we will carry out **reasonable and proportionate searches** across systems where relevant personal data is likely to be held. These may include, where applicable:

- management information systems;
- safeguarding and pastoral records;
- SEN and support files;

- email and shared storage systems;
- paper records and archives.

All information identified will be reviewed carefully to ensure compliance with data protection law, safeguarding duties, and thirdparty privacy obligations.

5. Safeguarding and ThirdParty Information

Please note that some information may be **redacted or withheld** where disclosure would:

- compromise safeguarding or child protection;
- reveal confidential sources;
- disclose personal data relating to other individuals; or
- cause serious harm to the physical or mental health of any person.

Where appropriate, information may be summarised rather than disclosed verbatim.

6. Format of Response

Our response will normally be provided in a **secure electronic format**, such as a passwordprotected PDF or secure portal.

If you require the information in an alternative accessible format, please let us know.

If you have any questions while your request is being processed, please contact **[DSAR Lead/DPO contact details]**, quoting the reference number above.

Yours sincerely,

[Name]
[Role]
[School/Trust/College]
[Contact details]

DATA SUBJECT ACCESS REQUEST - EXTENSION NOTICE (14)

[School/Trust/College Letterhead]

Date: [dd/mm/yyyy]
Private and Confidential

Dear [Name],

Notice of Extension - Data Subject Access Request

We write further to your **Data Subject Access Request ('DSAR')** received on **[date].**

We are writing to inform you that we require an extension of the statutory deadline to respond to your request, in accordance with **Article 12(3) of the UK General Data Protection Regulation.**

1. Statutory Basis for Extension

The UK GDPR allows organisations to extend the standard onemonth deadline by **up to two further months** where a request is complex or involves a significant volume of data.

Your request has been assessed as **complex**, and an extension is therefore necessary in order to ensure that your request is handled lawfully, accurately, and safely.

2. Reasons for Complexity

The complexity of your request arises from one or more of the following factors:

- the volume of personal data held across multiple education systems;
- the need to search historic records, email accounts, and shared storage locations;
- the presence of **mixed data** relating to multiple individuals;
- the involvement of **safeguarding, pastoral, or SEN records** requiring careful review;
- the need to apply redactions and consider lawful exemptions on a linebyline basis.

These factors require detailed review to ensure that disclosure is proportionate and that the rights and safety of all individuals are protected.

3. Revised Deadline

As a result, the deadline for responding to your DSAR has been extended.

- **Original deadline:** [date]
- **Extended deadline:** [date – up to two months later]

We will provide our full response **by the extended deadline set out above.**

4. Ongoing Processing of Your Request

We continue to process your request and are carrying out **reasonable and proportionate searches** across relevant systems.

All information identified will be reviewed carefully to:

- identify personal data relating to the data subject;
- protect the personal data of third parties;
- comply with safeguarding and child protection duties; and
- apply any relevant exemptions where lawful and necessary.

5. Your Rights

If you have any questions about this extension, please contact **[DSAR Lead/DPO contact details]**, quoting the reference number above.

If you are dissatisfied with the application of this extension, you have the right to complain to the **Information Commissioner's Office (ICO)**.

Further information about your rights is available at **www.ico.org.uk**.

Yours sincerely,

[Name]
[Role]
[School/Trust/College]
[Contact details]

Index

Information Commissioner's Office (ICO)

Mixed data

Multiagency information

Parental responsibility

Personal data

Redaction

Safeguarding

SEND records

Statutory timescales

Summaries

Templates and tools

Thirdparty data

UK GDPR
Articles 12 and 15

Data Subject Access Requests (DSARs) present unique and often highrisk challenges for schools, multiacademy trusts and colleges. Requests frequently arise in situations involving safeguarding concerns, parental disputes, SEND disagreements, staff grievances or regulatory scrutiny – where decisions about disclosure can have serious consequences for children, staff and institutions alike.

DSARs in Education is a practical safeguardingfocused guide designed specifically for education settings in England and Wales. It goes beyond generic GDPR guidance to address the realities schools face: mixed data involving children and families, sensitive safeguarding records, professional opinions, multiagency information and highconflict requests made under pressure.

Written for school leaders, data protection officers, designated safeguarding leads, SENCOs, HR teams and administrators, this guide provides clear, structured support on how to:

- identify what personal data is held in education settings
- manage mixed data and thirdparty information lawfully
- balance access rights against safeguarding duties
- apply exemptions confidently and proportionately
- document decisions so they are defensible if challenged
- communicate responses clearly, professionally and safely.

The book includes stepbystep workflows, decisionmaking frameworks, and a comprehensive suite of templates and tools to support consistent, auditable DSAR handling across schools, trusts and colleges.

This is not about defensive practice or withholding information. It is about **providing access responsibly, transparently and safely – with the welfare of children at the centre of every decision.**

Printed and bound by CPI Group (UK) Ltd, Croydon, CR0 4YY
14/07/2026
02166339-0001